LIFE AFTER SOUTHDOWN

FORMER BUSES IN SERVICE ELSEWHERE

LIFE AFTER
SOUTHDOWN
FORMER BUSES IN
SERVICE ELSEWHERE

SIMON STANFORD

AMBERLEY

First published 2020

Amberley Publishing
The Hill, Stroud
Gloucestershire, GL5 4EP

www.amberley-books.com

Copyright © Simon Stanford, 2020

The right of Simon Stanford to be identified as
the Author of this work has been asserted in
accordance with the Copyrights, Designs and
Patents Act 1988.

ISBN 978 1 4456 9599 0 (print)
ISBN 978 1 4456 9600 3 (ebook)

British Library Cataloguing in Publication Data.
A catalogue record for this book is available from
the British Library.

Origination by Amberley Publishing.
Printed in the UK.

Introduction

When Southdown buses and coaches were withdrawn from service, thus ending their passenger-carrying days on the south coast, they were normally sold to dealers, commonly in large numbers for onward sale to other operators for further service or to be converted to other uses such as driver training buses, cafés, play buses, exhibition buses, shops or even travellers' homes – their uses were endless. Those not so fortunate, deemed unfit for further use, would end up in the breakers yard and a sad end would be in sight. In my time working for Southdown from the late 1970s through to the 1980s I witnessed the mass cull of Leyland Leopards, Bristol REs and VRs, and the renowned Queen Mary double-deckers, seeing large batches collected from Southdown depots where many had been in storage pending disposal. They would then head north – some driven, some on tow to the dealers' yards – to await a new home or, much worse, the dreaded scrap man. During the National Bus Company era it was common to see transfers of vehicles between other NBC companies bringing Southdown buses and coaches to many other parts of the country. Some would change hands many times, becoming very well travelled indeed.

Southdown was a very well-respected company known for quality in the vehicles it operated, which had an added uniqueness. This, coupled with their high standards of maintenance and presentation, made them sought after, particularly by the small independent operator, with many sold for further use to companies all over the UK. It was never very difficult to spot an ex-Southdown bus when on one's travels. Not only were they snapped up by operators in this country, but Southdown buses could be seen worldwide. Queen Marys were snapped up by China Motor Bus, some went to Saudi Arabia, Dubai, Japan, New Jersey USA, Croatia, Germany ... the list is endless. Bristol VR double-deckers were popular in the Netherlands, while another VR is in Canada.

Not only did Southdown vehicles find themselves sold to operators all over this country and overseas, they went in large numbers too; for example, thirty Leyland Leopard buses went to East Kent, thirty Daimler Fleetlines went to Crosville, over thirty Leyland Leopards went to Ulsterbus to replace buses destroyed in troubled times, Rennies Coaches of Dunfermline took forty-seven Leyland Leopard coaches, and over 100 Leyland PD3 Queen Marys went overseas to Hong Kong and other far-flung places. When their service lives came to an end numerous buses and coaches were secured for preservation.

Life After Southdown is a pictorial tribute to vehicles once seen on the roads of towns and villages on the south coast, many in the traditional green and cream. Buses and coaches are shown after disposal with other operators, losing that familiar green in favour of different liveries and varied colour schemes, some changing identity completely. The era chosen for the book reflects not only my employment with Southdown, but also growing up in their operating area and my forty-plus years as an enthusiast.

I particularly wanted to include some examples of life after Southdown in preservation, with those preserved and lovingly restored to their original condition for us all to enjoy and remind us of the days when green and cream buses could be seen all over the south coast.

The British Shoe Corporation, based in Leicester, operated a fleet of buses and coaches for staff transport and favoured former Southdown vehicles. This impressive lineup is of nine Queen Marys and four Leyland PD2s, outnumbering the coach, which of course is not a Southdown.

A new life and a new identity. Queen Mary 6928 CD joined many others in the China Motor Bus fleet, coping admirably with the change in climate compared with their lives on the south coast of England. PD506 was her fleet number and, having undergone a major rebuild to half-cab form in 1983, she was withdrawn and scrapped in 1987. (Courtesy of Paul Olgivie)

New to Southdown in 1962 is this Commer Avenger coach with bodywork by Harrington of Hove. Photographed in Newark bus station and under ownership of Alex Smith Coachways of Beeston.

Weymann-bodied Leyland Leopard 1164. One of a large number of former Southdown coaches to be operated by Hants & Dorset, she became their fleet No. 3094.

Weymann-bodied Leyland Leopard 1166. One of a number of former Southdown coaches owned by Wimpey Construction to convey workers to construction sites. (Courtesy of Bristol Vintage Bus Group)

1180 is a Leyland Leopard with Plaxton Panorama coachwork – new in 1964. Looking very smart indeed with Cresta Coaches of Bridgend. It is believed that this rare coach still survives today.

Formerly a playbus, this Harrington Cavalier 1708 has been converted to a mobile caravan in this view from 1987. It is reported to have been still in use as late as 2009. (Courtesy of Nigel Lukowski)

The varied life of Harrington Grenadier 1750 after Southdown saw her in Suffolk with Bickers coaches. Here she finds herself in Scotland with Classique Coaches looking superb and still in Southdown traditional green. She was photographed here in 1994 at Loch Long, Argyllshire, and is still active today in preservation. (Courtesy of Stuart Little)

Harrington-bodied Leyland Leopard 1752 looking rather tired since her Southdown days. Photographed in Worthing, May 1983, still carrying the identity of her previous owner – Dan-Air Engineering. (Courtesy of Nigel Lukowski)

Former 1739 in royal blue livery, the coaching division of Western National. Seen here at Salisbury in 1973. This Harrington coach had continued fame when EFE made a model of it in 2005. (Courtesy of Colin L. Caddy)

Many buses and coaches had a new lease of life carrying private groups. Harrington coach 1760 was owned by the Congleton Scout Group when photographed here in 1987. (Courtesy of Nigel Lukowski)

New to Brighton, Hove & District in 1962 and spending subsequent years with Southdown is Bristol Lodekka XPM 42, seen here with Lincolnshire Road Car Company. This 1980 view is taken in Skegness. She later became AFE 171A, with the original registration being transferred to a coach.

Another former Southdown Bristol Lodekka new to Brighton, Hove & District is 2064. It seems it was no longer in use when photographed here in 1984 at Llanfaethlu. (Courtesy of Nigel Lukowski)

The Queen Mary was a popular bus for independent operators in the north-east. OK Motor Services from County Durham bought seven, looking smart in their livery and clearly well cared for. XUF 848 and XUF 849 were two of the older ones seen here in 1975. (Courtesy of Stuart Little)

Leyland PD3s, or Queen Marys as they were fondly referred to, were snapped up by new owners worldwide. Only a handful of the 285-strong fleet did not find new homes. Former 960 CUF, now HOO 343B, was photographed in the West Midlands as a driver training bus.

A black and white view of Queen Mary 250, a driver training bus with Northern General. New in 1965, she is looking similar to her Southdown days (still in National Bus Company green and white) but with her new owner's fleet names.

Many Queen Marys found themselves with new lives as driver training buses. No. 253 was with Northern General when this view was taken in 1986.

Looking very smart indeed, here is Queen Mary 261 – new in 1965. Photographed in Northampton, June 1982, with Brittain's Coaches. (Courtesy of Nigel Lukowski)

BUF 272C is seen here in 1984, in the fleet of Confidence coaches, Leicestershire, who operated several ex-Southdown vehicles. No. 272 was owned by them for around fifteen years and has now returned to Southdown green and cream livery in preservation, back home in Sussex.

Queen Mary 272, a bus with a busy life after service with Southdown. Wearing a green and cream livery with 'Firebond insurance specialists' upon it, it is used as a publicity vehicle in the Cambridgeshire area.

Queen Mary 275 was used in and around London by Lambeth Borough Council as their consumer bus. It is seen here in Vauxhall, South London, in May 1984.

Many Southdown vehicles have had a chequered history and 278 is no exception. Photographed here with Boroline of Maidstone as their fleet No. 290, she was used for driver training as well as a passenger-carrying service. She was once reregistered to 217 UKL, but is now BUF 278C again and joining fellow Queen Marys in preservation.

BUF 278C, reunited with her original registration and restored to green and cream, is seen here proudly on display at a bus rally in Merthyr Tydfil, 2010.

Queen Mary FCD 295D spent some of her Southdown career as a driver training bus in yellow. After disposal she continued this role with Shamrock & Rambler before becoming part of the North Western training fleet. Bootle bus station is the location in this 1991 image. (Courtesy of Paul Green)

Instantly recognisable as a Southdown Queen Mary, this view of FCD 311D was taken in Portree, Isle of Skye, in June 1982. She was withdrawn in 1983 and is reported to have been the only double-decker in use there at that time. (Courtesy of Stuart Little)

Queen Mary 358 had a new life, similar to others of this batch, as a driver trainer. She is seen here retaining some of the green livery. She ended her days in Scotland with Rennies of Dunfermline, continuing the training role.

Queen Mary 362 spent many years as a driver trainer with Southdown and continued this role in Scotland with Midland Bluebird.

Many innovative ways have been found to put buses and coaches to good use after their passenger-carrying days have ended. Queen Mary 366 was converted to partial open top and used as a mobile bowling alley. Photographed around 1987.

400 DCD was numerically the first of thirty convertible, open-top Queen Marys. After service with Southdown she was photographed in 1989 with Stagecoach in Cumberland, intended as a driver trainer. She was never used and was sadly scrapped, donating her registration to a Stagecoach bus.

Formerly 410 DCD, though nicknamed 'Bertie', this bus is looking splendid in London Pride sightseeing livery after being reregistered to BHM 288. I cannot be precise with the date other than I took a trip to London in the 1990s luckily armed with a camera. No. 410 survives today in preservation, reunited with her original registration and returned to original green and cream.

PRX 189B was originally 417 DCD with Southdown and is photographed with Cleveland Transit in a striking yellow and green livery, becoming fleet No. 500. She was used on a variety of work around the Hartlepool area before returning south to join other Queen Marys in preservation and returning to original green and cream.

Queen Mary 419 left the Southdown fleet for a driver training career with Trent, reregistered DRR 153B. After disposal she was fortunate enough to return home to the south in the hands of preservationists and regain her original registration of 419 DCD. This August 2019 photo at Tinkers Park Bus Rally in East Sussex shows her looking resplendent in all-over white with her present owner from Newhaven, MWH Commercials. (Courtesy of Steve Hearn)

After sale by Southdown, permanent open-top Queen Mary 427 was used as a promotional vehicle by a number of businesses. Photographed at the 1988 Epsom Derby, certainly no stranger to this event, she is seen in all-over-red livery. (Courtesy of Alan Conway)

No. 427 is seen here at Donnington in 1991 continuing her publicity vehicle role. She has had a change of colour to a rather dull green, a far cry from the Southdown traditional livery she once wore. Around 2008 was the end for No. 427 when she returned to Sussex and no doubt donated parts to keep other buses going before being scrapped. (Courtesy of Simon Beeston)

Queen Mary BUF 429C was withdrawn by Southdown in 1978 and is photographed here in a Yorkshire dealer's yard around a year or so later. She eventually ended up in Croatia around 1998 in a yellow livery, advertising a local beer and joining many other buses from the UK.

AOR 157B, originally 422 DCD, was used in the early 1990s by Leisurelink on the summer No. 17 service. This photo was taken along Maderia Drive, Brighton. No. 422 is another Queen Mary fortunate to join others in preservation.

A rear view of 277 AUF – the bus on the front cover. Formerly No. 677 with Southdown, this view shows the Marshall-bodied Leyland Leopard in the East Kent fleet.

East Kent Road Car Company operated many former Southdown Leyland Leopards with Marshall bodywork. No. 101 is seen here with another Southdown Leyland Leopard, No. 670, seen on the left.

This 1963 batch of former Southdown Marshall-bodied Leyland Leopards were sold to East Kent for new lives in the Folkestone area of Kent. No. 670 was photographed here around 1974. (Courtesy of Brian Weeden)

After having operated for East Kent along with other Leopards from this batch, No. 673 was sold to Rules of Boxford in Suffolk. She is now beautifully preserved in East Kent livery, as seen here at Tinkers Park Bus Rally in 2018. Remarkably, she is fifty-five years old.

A superb rear view of this remarkable survivor in 2018. I had a ride on her during the Tinkers Park running day and a photo stop was essential in the east Sussex countryside on this bright and sunny day.

Leopard 679 with East Kent in Dover. She had continued service after leaving Kent and operated in Scotland for Rapson of Brora in the Scottish Highlands. (Courtesy of Brian Weeden)

Back to the Folkestone area where No. 682 was photographed in 1974. She was another Leopard from this batch to see further service after East Kent with the independent Berresfords of Cheddleton. (Courtesy of Brian Weeden)

A 1975 view of No. 683 taken in the Ashford area. After withdrawal by East Kent in 1976, she was bought by a Leicestershire operator and found fame in 1977 after being painted in the Queen's Silver Jubilee livery. (Courtesy of Brian Weeden)

Canterbury 1971 is the setting for Leyland leopard 684 with East Kent. (Courtesy of Stuart Little)

Leopard 107 had a varied career after Southdown. This view shows her with Heyfordian Travel from Oxforshire in 1980. She also served with an operator in Swansea. (Courtesy of Nigel Lukowski)

Former Southdown single-deckers were popular second-hand acquisitions for Heyfordian Travel, having both Leyland and Bristol examples. Leopard 112 is seen here, at their premises in 1982, carrying all-over-white livery. (Courtesy of Nigel Lukowski)

Marshall-bodied Leopard 127 is seen here in the Stanley Gath fleet based in Yorkshire. Just visible in this view is No. 152, another Leopard carrying Weymann bodywork.

114 CUF, a Marshall-bodied Leyland Leopard, is photographed here in 1983. She became part of the Tally Ho! fleet from Kingsbridge, Devon. (Courtesy of Nigel Lukowski)

No. 140, a Weymann-bodied Leopard with Aspden's of Blackburn. She was for sale when I photographed her at Aspden's premises in Blackburn. Unfortunately, she did not find a new owner and was sadly scrapped.

Stokes of Carstairs, Lanarkshire, started in around 1925 and operated until around 2010. They were one of many small independent operators to favour the Leyland Leopard, particularly former Southdown examples. With Weymann bodywork, No. 153 is photographed at their premises.

No. 231 is a Bristol RE-bodied bus by Marshall of Cambridge. Southdown owned forty of these forty-five-seat buses dating from 1968, and only a handful had further lives after Southdown had finished with them. This Bristol had operated in Wales before working as the Beeches courtesy bus in the Rotherham area. (Courtesy of Garry Donnelly)

Seen with Butlers of Loughborough, here is another Bristol RE. No. 241 is seen still wearing Southdown National green – very much the same livery as when it was withdrawn by Southdown. (Courtesy of Joe Gornall)

From a batch of twenty longer forty-nine-seat Marshall-bodied Bristol Res, with just over half seeing further service after withdrawal. Numerically the first, No. 430 is seen here in 1982 and joined seven others from the batch to operate with Heyfordian Travel in Oxfordshire. (Courtesy of Nigel Lukowski)

A 1982 black and white view of Bristol RE 434 with Heyfordian Travel. Regrettably, none of this batch have survived in preservation.

Bristol 437 is seen here in Oxfordshire in 1982 at Heyfordian Travel's premises, showing off her smart all-over-white livery. I have seen this Bristol in a red livery, and she apparently saw further service as a film crew bus. (courtesy of Nigel Lukowski)

SZY 587, Northern Counties-bodied Leyland Leopard PUF 165H, found a new life in Ireland. My visit to O'Sullivans Coaches in County Limerick, Ireland, sometime in the early 1990s revealed this rare find looking rather down at heel. Luckily it was rescued and returned to Sussex to be reunited with her original registration and restored.

This bus is from a batch of thirty rather unique Leyland Leopards with bodywork by Northern Counties. Only around half of these saw further service after withdrawal by Southdown. Some were put to good use in Wales – notably by Hills of Tredegar. No. 473 is seen here with Eynon's of Trimsaran in 1990, looking as though her days are numbered. (Courtesy of Paul Green)

No. 481, from a small batch of Bristol REs and new in 1971, saw service with operators not too far from her original Sussex home. This 1991 photo is taken in Ashford with Kent Coach Tours. No. 481 still survives in preservation. (Courtesy of Paul Ogilvie)

New in 1966, EUF 192D was from a large number of Leyland Leopards bodied by Plaxton. She is seen here in 1979 enjoying a new life in the West Country with Willis of Bodmin in Cornwall. (Courtesy of Nigel Lukowski)

Retiring to the West Country and seen in Torquay in 1981 is No. 1201, another Leopard with Plaxton coachwork, now owned by the Wakefield Majorettes. (Courtesy of Nigel Lukowski)

Leyland Leopard 1785, with Duple Commander coachwork in a very uninspiring black colour scheme, stayed close to home in her new life. She is seen here in Hove. (Courtesy of Nigel Lukowski)

Here is London's Victoria coach station in 1982. No. 1228, owned by Sherrin's coaches from Carhampton in Somerset, would have been no stranger to London in her Southdown days. (Courtesy of Nigel Lukowski)

Photographed in Blaneau Festiniog on a rather wet and gloomy day in September 1986 is Leyland Leopard coach No. 1231. (Courtesy of Nigel Lukowski)

RUF 800H was numerically the first of a batch of twenty Leyland Leopards with Duple Commander bodywork. No. 1800 passed to Alder Valley around 1975 – seen here in National white. This coach also operated in Reading to Heathrow railair livery.

With little change since her Southdown days, No. 1820 is one of a pair of Plaxton Elite-bodied Leopards acquired by Maidstone & District and East Kent around 1976. (Courtesy of M&D and East Kent Bus Club)

Sister No. 1821 was loaned to M&D from East Kent and is seen here working an express service to Dover. (Courtesy of M&D and East Kent Bus Club)

After working for several coach firms, having two registration number changes and gaining a Supreme front grille, it is pleasing to see No. 1835 from the 1971 batch of Plaxton Elite-bodied Leyland Leopards preserved and appearing at the Southdown Centenary in 2015. She has been aptly named the 'Eastbourne Pullman' as she spent most of her Southdown career at Eastbourne depot.

PPM 210G, photographed at Southsea, is a Bristol RE bodied by ECW in dual-door form new to Brighton, Hove & District in 1968 and transferred to Southdown around 1969. Sherrin's of Carhampton in Somerset owned her for around six years. No. 2210 survives in preservation and is superbly restored in NBC green.

After Crosville withdrew the former Southdown Daimler Fleetlines many saw further service around the country. No. 371 is seen here in May 1985 at Clydebank with Duncan Stewart Coaches. (Courtesy of Stuart Little)

In open-top happy dragon green, white and yellow striking livery is Daimler Fleetline 375 with Crosville as their HDG 905. This view is at Old Colwyn in June 1987.

Thirty Southdown Daimler Fleetlines were acquired by Crosville in the early 1980s and operated in a variety of liveries, with many converted to open-top form. No. 376 is one of the Northern Counties examples. (Courtesy of Wessex Transport Society)

Former No. 385 is one of the Daimler Fleetlines bodied by Eastern coachworks. She is photographed here at Crosville Edge Lane depot in 1984. She had continued service in Lincolnshire after withdrawal by Crosville and was scrapped around 1990. (Courtesy of Nigel Lukowski)

Fleet No. HDL926 with Crosville in 1981 is Daimler Fleetline XUF 396K, looking very similar to her Southdown days when photographed in Chester. (Courtesy of Nigel Lukowski)

Around a dozen early Bristol VR double-deckers from Southdown joined the Daimlers in around 1981 with Crosville. At rest in between journeys we see No. 507, complete with National Holidays advertising between decks. (Courtesy of Nigel Lukowski)

Sisters again. Here we see former Southdown Bristol VR 508 carrying fleet No. DVG550 with her new owner, Crosville, branded for BWS Gwynedd working service 62 to Amlwch in North Wales. (Courtesy of Wessex Transport Society)

Bristol VR 512 passed to Brighton and Hove in January 1986. She is seen here in the November of that year in Old Steine Brighton, looking smart in her new owner's fleet colours. Cambridgeshire was her next county to operate in after Sussex, being scrapped around 1996. (Courtesy of Nigel Lukowski)

Another batch of Bristol VRs to leave Southdown in 1982 were ten of the dual-door examples finding a home with Bristol Omnibus Company. Former WUF 528K is No. 5201 with her new owner.

Dare I say it, we have sisters again. No. 529 with Bristol Cityline looking similar to how I remembered these buses in Brighton. These twin-door VRs would serve Bristol for around four years.

The early 1980s saw the second batch of Daimler Fleetlines to find new homes. These were the Northern Counties dual-door buses new to Brighton, Hove & District. Maidstone & District and East Kent bought them, and a variety of liveries and modifications would follow. No. 2103 is photographed here in Dover in NBC green. (Courtesy of M&D and East Kent Bus Club)

No. 2016 is seen in Dover with East Kent with its exit door removed and modified destination apertures. This bus brings back memories for me, having seen service with Southdown in Haywards Heath. (Courtesy of M&D and East Kent Bus Club)

Retaining the exit door and original destination aperture, former No. 2114 has been photographed here in Dover in 1987, now with East Kent and numbered 7314. Hoverspeed livery is one of a multitude of liveries for these fleetlines.

With modified destination and East Kent fleet names, this shot of No. 2122 was taken in Dover. The exit doors were removed and seating capacity was increased on these buses for normal service work. (Courtesy of M&D and East Kent Bus Club)

No. 2125 is seen here in all-over-red livery working a Townsend Thoresen contract. She also wore a P&O Ferries blue-based livery for East Kent. (Courtesy of M&D and East Kent Bus Club)

No. 2126 is seen here in an attractive livery operating the Canterbury city sightseeing tour for East Kent, carrying their fleet No. 7326. (Courtesy of M&D and East Kent Bus Club)

Southdown owned thirty-seven Ford coaches new in 1974. After disposal many saw further service with the small independent coach operator. No. 1408 was photographed in Torquay in April 1983 with Carlton Tours. (Courtesy of Nigel Lukowski)

Ford 1409 was a very well-travelled coach, working for a number of firms. She is seen here with Kestrel Coaches, Llandudno, in September 1985. (Courtesy of Nigel Lukowski)

Like many batches of former Southdown buses and coaches, they become distant memories for those of us that remember them only too well with Southdown. No. 1409, now forty-five years old, still survives in the north of Scotland with Maynes Coaches, although it is no longer in use.

Formerly PUF 254M in the Southdown fleet, this Ford Duple coach was reregistered to SZY 741 when photographed here in 1984 at Rock Ferry in the Anchor Tours fleet. (Courtesy of Nigel Lukowski)

With Huxley of Malpas, Cheshire, is Ford coach No. 1417 working a stage carriage service here in Chester in 1987. (Courtesy of Nigel Lukowski)

Looking smart in the Williams Coaches fleet is Ford Duple PUF 262M, formerly No. 1422 with Southdown. This 1986 photo was taken in Blackpool. (Courtesy of Nigel Lukowski)

Ford Duple coach No. 1430 returned home to Brighton in August 1980 on a day trip with her new owner, Hants & Dorset. (Courtesy of Nigel Lukowski)

Another small coach operator, Pyes, operated ex-Southdown Ford No. 1437 in plain white livery. Llandudno is the location for this image, taken in 1984. (Courtesy of Nigel Lukowski)

Leyland Atlantean 710 (one from the batch once owned by Ribble) is seen in the Ensign yard in June 1992. An addition to the list of former Southdown buses used as a driver training bus.

Many of the forty-seven-strong batch of Southdown Leyland Atlanteans found new homes in the north of England. No. 717 was operated by Pennine Blue and Ribble, and is seen here in Hyde, Manchester, in 1991 still in Ribble livery.

During my time working for London Country I was fortunate enough to see the former Southdown Atlanteans still in service and had opportunities to take the odd photo or two. No. 723 was AN302 with LCBS and commonly used on the 127 Purley to Tooting service.

The former Southdown Leyland Atlanteans fitted in well with London Country's own fleet of this type. AN305 is at Chelsham depot in 1989.

Leyland Atlantean 733 saw service with London Country after Southdown and joined others from the batch to operate in the Manchester area with the Bee Line Buzz Company.

Another of the Atlantean batch to serve Manchester is No. 739 in the attractive two-tone blue of Citibus – one of four used by this operator.

A black and white view of former No. 741 with London Country. The Southdown Atlanteans served with LCBS for around four years until sold to a dealer in around 1989.

A rear view of No. 741. The Southdown Atlanteans in service with London Country were normally to be found allocated to service 127.

Leyland National BCD 808L was to take on a complete new identity, as seen here with Midland Fox in Leicester prior to becoming one of many Leyland Nationals rebuilt to a National Greenway in 1994 – a combined London Country and East Lancs project. She was registered to JIL 2197, serving with London & Country and Arriva.

Leyland National BCD 822L was fleet no. 22 with Southdown – one of twenty-five new in 1973. Seen here with Kingsman Travel of Sheffield in the early 1990s.

Another South Wales operator to purchase former Southdown buses was Glyn Williams. Leyland National 23, dating from 1973, looks smart in green and white. She was withdrawn from service and scrapped around 1998, giving twenty-five years of sterling service.

Following her withdrawal by Southdown Leyland National, No. 37 had operated for Provincial in Hampshire and Rennies of Dunfermline in Scotland. She is seen here restored and preserved when photographed at the Cobham Bus Rally in 2009.

Birmingham Coach Company operated a large fleet of second-hand Leyland Nationals for their services in and around the West Midlands, including former Southdown examples. RUF 41R is route branded for service 410. (Courtesy of Peter Scott)

Leyland National 51 was bought by Panther Buses, a rather short-lived operator trying to compete with London Country. She is seen here loading passengers in Crawley bus station around 1991.

National 58 is seen here close to the Crawley depot in plain white, in service with London & Country subsidiary Gem Fairtax. She ended up with an operator in Scotland before the final trip to the scrap man in 2003.

I was lucky enough to be among a few former Southdown Nationals as well as Atlanteans in my London Country days. Freshly adorned in an all-over-advert livery near to Crawley bus garage, No. 60 had Gem Fairtax fleet names – an offshoot of London Country.

Gem Fairtax ceased to operate in the late 1990s. 60 continued her life after Southdown and looked very smart indeed in London & Country livery.

In service with the Birmingham Coach Company after disposal by Brighton and Hove is new to Southdown Leyland National number 66. Still in Brighton & Hove livery, the Conway Street depot allocation disc is still displayed in the windscreen.

Stagecoach acquired Southdown in 1989 and the fleet was repainted in their corporate livery. Eastbourne depot is the location for Leyland National 69. (Courtesy of Bristol Vintage Bus Group)

A bus familiar to me when I worked for Southdown at Haywards Heath depot was Leyland National 72. She took some tracking down in her new life in Liverpool with CMT buses.

Leyland National 75 had a long life after Southdown with P&O Ferries at Dover as a courtesy bus before being acquired for preservation and repainting in National Bus Company green and white. This view was taken at Showbus Rally in 2008.

Another bus I remember well during my time with Southdown in Haywards Heath was Leyland National 95. Looking down at heel and presumably withdrawn from service, this photo was taken in 2001 in the Fife area of Scotland. (Courtesy of Alan Conway)

Another former Southdown National to operate in the Birmingham area still in Brighton & Hove livery was AYJ 106T.

National 118, numerically the last of the Mk I Nationals new to Southdown. It was in the ownership of Sussex Coaches when it was photographed in Guildford in 1999. The 89 would have been the Haywards Heath to Horsham service. (Courtesy of Alan Conway)

A Mk II Leyland National new to Southdown in 1980, passing to Brighton & Hove in 1986, is seen here with a Wycombe bus. After service there, No. 128 saw further service in Lincolnshire.

Bristol VR 553 became L147 in the Hedingham Omnibus fleet in Essex and was based in Clacton-on-Sea. She lasted with this operator until around 2000.

No. 556 was a well-travelled Bristol VR, leaving Southdown to join the Ribble fleet for around three years, then moving to Essex with 'Stephenson's' appearing in an all-over-advert livery. Finally, she was converted to a non-PSV mobile display/shop as depicted in this view. She would end her days in Ireland before being scrapped.

Bristol VR No. 557 passed to Black Horse Buses of Gravesend, seen here in 1990 painted in their attractive orange and silver livery. She only stayed a short time with this operator, being scrapped in 1993.

This view of Bristol VR former Southdown 571 became DVG593 in the fleet of Crosville Wales after withdrawal by Brighton and Hove. After Crosville had finished with her, she ended her days with Price Coaches before being scrapped in 1996. This view was taken in Wrexham in 1989. (Courtesy of Nigel Lukowski)

Bristol VR 589 had a dramatic end to her life after Southdown. From Brighton and Hove she was bought by Thornton Dale Coaches from Pickering, Yorkshire, and blown over in a storm in 1992 then scrapped soon after.

Ryans of Bath's pair of dual-door, convertible, open-top Bristol VR buses were used for the Bath sightseeing tour. Photographed with their roofs in place.

The convertible open-top Bristol VR double-deckers were popular with a variety of operators after sale by Southdown. No. 596 is seen here in Bath with Ryans on city sightseeing duties in open-top form.

One of many former Southdown vehicles to have a new life abroad is Bristol VR SNJ 590R, seen here in Willenstad, Netherlands, in 2016. She was exported here in 2004, but was never registered. She is in static use with Sauna Diana. (Courtesy of Frans Angevaare)

SNJ 591R was operated by Hedingham in Essex before finding a new life in the Netherlands to join sister 590. Arriving here in 2006, but not registered, she is in static use as a holiday cottage. This recent photograph shows her new life in Vuren. (Courtesy of Frans Angevaare)

When security was not as stringent as nowadays, trips around Sellafield nuclear power station were operated by open-top bus. Bristol VR UWV 610S is seen here in full Sellafield Visitor Centre colours around 1988.

Former UWV 612S, a convertible open-top Bristol VR, joins the ranks of buses living abroad in their new lives. She is now registered BN-XD-80 in the Netherlands and used as a publicity bus. Photographed in Sliedrecht in 2006. (Courtesy of Frans Angevaare)

Frankie, a former Southdown convertible open-top Bristol VR enjoying retirement in Devon, albeit an active one. No. 614 was previously used on service 100, the rail river link. She is now preserved in that smart livery. Seen here posing for the camera on Sunday 25 August 2019 at the waterside, Plymouth.

A rear shot of *Frankie* at Plymouth, taking part in the Plymouth Bus Rally and still retaining the advertising from her open-top service days.

A well-travelled No. 618. Another from the batch of twenty-nine convertible open-top Bristol VRs. Seen here in the Lake District in May 2000 at Grasmere, working a sightseeing tour for Sellafield nuclear power station. She also carried the Lakeland Experience livery and travelled onward to Essex to carry sightseers on Southend seafront. Around 2005 she was exported to New Jersey, USA, where she was used by an American football team. (Courtesy of Alan Conway)

UWV 620S (registered BR-ZP-37 in 2006) is seen here at Hengelo, Netherlands, in 2018. She is photographed out of use here, but served as a publicity bus connected with paintball, as the advertising depicts. (Courtesy of Frans Angevaare)

Bristol VR 623 was in open-top form for much of her life after Southdown, although she has been reunited with her roof on occasions. Since Southdown, Guide Friday used her in Hastings for their open-top sightseeing tour; similarly, she operated the Whitby town tour. In this view, taken at the Worthing Bus Rally in 2011, she has returned south under Morton's Coaches from Hampshire ownership.

Bristol VR 251 ended her passenger-carrying days as a tree lopper with Stagecoach. Southdown centenary at Southsea is the location for this photo, which was taken in 2015.

JWV 259W was a 1981 Bristol VR and embarked on a new life in idyllic Cornwall. She had a sad ending, though, being destroyed in a fire at its owners depot in 2013. An immaculate 259 was photographed in Newquay 2010 in her third livery with Western Greyhound. (Courtesy of Alan Conway)

Looking in fine fettle is Leyland Leopard 1254 with Duple Dominant coachwork, photographed in the West Midlands with operator T&T Travel. This view is from 1989. (Courtesy of Paul Green)

After withdrawal by Southdown, batches of vehicles would end up in dealers' yards awaiting new owners or a much sadder ending. Duple-bodied Leyland Leopard 1256 is seen with a dealer in 1986 devoid of her Southdown East and Mid Sussex fleet names. She had a new life in Northern Ireland reregistered to ADZ 9332. (Courtesy of A&R Photos)

Scottish operator Rennies of Dunfermline purchased around forty-seven Leyland Leopard coaches with Plaxton and Duple bodywork from Southdown. They were all of varying ages and were ran in a variety of liveries. No. 1268, new in 1976, is seen here in a red and white livery.

Leyland Leopard Plaxton fleet No. 1271, new to Southdown in 1976, could not settle down it would seem, having somewhere around eight owners before the dreaded scrap man got hold of her in 1997. S&P coaches was the operator in this view from around 1991.

Former OWV 277R is seen here in Rennies livery and fleet names with a new identity as IIW 8815 – her fourth registration. She was sold by Rennies in 1996 to become one of several to see continued service in Scotland.

YYJ 298T was one of the 12-metre Plaxton-bodied Leopard coaches acquired by Rennies. She is seen here with fleet names, but only had them for a year, staying in Scotland with Bairds Coaches. She ended up in Northern Ireland as 79-DL-664 where she ended her days.

Formerly YYJ 302T and losing her original identity to become FRX 869T, this is another addition to the Rennies of Dunfermline fleet of former Southdown Leyland Leopards.

No. 1304 had a short stay in Scotland with Rennies and was acquired by Blackburn Transport around 1988. She is seen here working a service to Bury.

Another Plaxton-bodied Leopard to leave Scotland after a short stay with Rennies was No. 1311, joining others from this batch to operate in Lancashire for Blackburn Transport.

No. 1321 was new as EAP 921V with Southdown, and became OPV 821 during her coaching career on the south coast. This March 1992 view in Hamilton shows her in the Mitchells Coaches fleet of Broxburn.

No. 1335 retained her original registration despite having a new life with several operators. She is seen here with Thornton Dale Coaches in North Yorkshire. East Yorkshire motor services and Ambassador Travel in Great Yarmouth once owned this coach.

Formerly EAP 937V with Southdown is this Leyland Leopard. She is seen here with Duple Dominant coachwork and in Maghull Coaches of Bootle livery when this shot was taken at the 2005 show bus rally. She has now been restored to National white livery and reunited with her original registration.

Leyland Leopard Plaxton Supreme in the fleet of Cyril Evans of Senghenydd, South Wales, is operating a stage carriage service to Caerphilly. She is looking tidy in the red and cream livery and no doubt at home among several other Leylands bought second hand by her new owner.

Another identity change for Plaxton-bodied Leyland Leopard 1355, new as LPN 355W, a 12-metre coach with Southdown. This 1989 view shows her as HSU 247 with Grampian Express coaches.

Another coach to receive the registration number from a Queen Mary is former 1364 HHC 364Y, a Plaxton Supreme-bodied Leyland Leopard seen here in the early 1990s in Hastings Coaches livery at their local depot under Stagecoach ownership.

A well-travelled Tiger. Formerly XUF 535Y and acquired by Stagecoach with the purchase of Southdown, she operated for Hampshire Bus and Stagecoach Western in Scotland and coach operators in High Wycombe, clocking up around seven owners since new and four registration numbers. I caught up with No. 1005 at a dealer's yard in Surrey.

New lives for former Southdown vehicles were often non-PSV use. Leyland Tiger A808 CCD, reregistered to A476 NJK, ended her passenger-carrying days as a café in Abercarn, South Wales. Seen here in 2009. (Courtesy of Paul Green)

I owned Leyland Tiger 1011 for eight years. Her life in preservation included restoration back to the National Holidays livery she wore when new in 1984. This image was taken at Detling Showground, Kent, in 2012.

It is hard to believe this is Leyland Tiger 1011. She appears here in her new guise as a Trent coach and reregistered to A10 CNU, continuing her life in preservation, albeit away from her original home in the south. This 2018 shot was taken at Donnington. (Courtesy of Simon Beeston)

HIG 4462 is a Volvo with Northern Counties bodywork from a batch of twelve purchased by Southdown – their last new buses. She was originally registered F308 MYJ. After her time with Stagecoach had ended, Sun Fun from the Cambridge area operated her in all-over-yellow livery, as seen in this shot taken in Southsea in preservationist ownership. She has now returned to the original Southdown green livery she wore when new.

After use by Stagecoach in Scotland, Volvo 312 returned south, purchased by operator Wiltax who was based in Surrey. Seen here at Showbus Rally, Duxford, in 2007, smartly turned out in their orange-based livery.

Once their lives after Southdown are over and they have gone to the big bus station in the sky, former Southdown buses have lived on in another form by donation of their registration number. 109 CUF originally belonged to a Marshall-bodied Leyland Leopard and was in the fleet of Silcox coaches of Pembroke in the late 1970s. A Silcox DAF Plaxton is seen in this view as 109 CUF.

Another Leyland Leopard to donate her registration and, ironically, also once operated by Silcox is 115 CUF, seen here carried on a Duple coach in the fleet of Ausden Clark.

Heavily cannibalised and vandalised is Northern Counties Leyland Leopard, having reached the end of her life with Hills of Tredegar. I recall my visit to South Wales around the late 1980s – much too late to see 476 complete and in service.

The Yorkshire scrapyards are where all buses – well, most anyway – end their lives. Queen Mary 364 served a useful life after Southdown as a training bus with Alder Valley. Photographed here around 1994, she had given twenty-eight years' service – a youthful end compared to some lucky to survive in preservation.

Queen Mary 286 lives on in preservation after a former driver training career with Northumbria and service with the erstwhile OK motor services of County Durham. Since her 2015 appearance at the Southdown centenary event in Southsea, she has been restored to OK livery – a fitting tribute.

Another preserved Queen Mary to attend the Southsea Rally in 2015 is Queen Mary 356, a former Confidence of Leicester bus operated by them in the early 1980s and still in their livery, with the Southdown green in evidence.

Bristol VR 583 passed to Brighton and Hove in 1986. From there she was converted to non-PSV use as a road safety unit in Birkenhead. Acquired for preservation and restoration when seen at Southsea in 2015, she is now fully beautifully restored to the National Bus Company livery she wore when new to Southdown.

Last but not least, the delightful No. 1141, new to Southdown in 1960, was fitted with Weymann fanfare coachwork and survived in preservation and was a regular rally attendee. Heyfordian once operated this coach, along with various others over the years. Oxford diecast have made a model of her adding to the model collections of Southdown enthusiasts.

Southdown Lives on at Amberley Museum

Amberley Museum is located in the South Downs National Park, close to Arundel in west Sussex. A former chalk quarry set in 36 acres is home to around eight former Southdown vehicles – some owned by the museum and some loaned. In addition to the vehicles there are two reconstructed Southdown garages, offices, a workshop and waiting room with a host of Southdown memorabilia too. Twice yearly – in spring and autumn – a bus event takes place with visiting buses and coaches. A fitting end to the book, with a selection of buses on display and giving rides around the museum grounds – a tribute to this wonderful museum. My thanks to the museum curator for permission to publish these photographs.

Front view of UF 7428, a 1931 Leyland Titan TD1. Parked over the inspection pit.

A rear view of UF 7428. The attention to detail on this bus and many other restored former Southdown vehicles is astonishing.

A general view of the museum bus-running day: UF 6473, a 1930 Leyland Titan, is seen giving rides around the grounds and the remarkable bus in the foreground, a Tilling Stevens, dates from 1914.

Much-travelled Bristol VR 516 was one of many in use with Crosville after Southdown. Her varied career continued when she was in permanent open-top use by crews maintaining the Mersey Tunnel. Restoration included roof replacement.

From a batch of ten Bristol RE buses with Leyland engines dating from 1971. No. 481 is one of two in preservation and is seen here giving rides around the museum, followed by a Willowbrook-bodied Leyland Leopard.

Bristol VR UWV 617S saw service in Scotland and Newquay before being purchased for preservation and restoration to Southdown West Sussex livery.

Two former Southdown Queen Mary registration numbers live on with Stagecoach. 404 DCD received a green and grey livery to represent the wartime livery carried by Southdown buses – part of the centenary celebrations in 2015. 403 DCD received 100 years of Southdown paintwork and graphics in the same year. Both buses are proudly on display at Amberley Museum.

Acknowledgements

I would like to express my thanks to a number of fellow enthusiasts who have helped me with photographs, slides and negatives to include in this book. While many images included have come from my own collection, numerous people have been only too happy to assist me with the use of their own material or have helped identify original photographers or given me some archive information, dates and locations. In particular, a huge thank you goes to Nigel Lukowski, Frans Angevaare for the Bristol VR images from the Netherlands, Brian Weedon from the Maidstone and District Enthusiasts Club, Paul Green, Stuart Little, Paul Webber, Bristol Vintage Bus Group, Alan Conway, Paul Gainsbury, Garry Donnelly, Joe Gornall, Wessex Transport Society, Peter Scott, Simon Beeston, Paul Olgivie, Steve Hearn, Richard Maryan, A & R Photos, and the late Colin L. Caddy. Sincere apologies if I have missed anyone out, and a very many thanks to you all.